Think Like an Athlete

TO CLARE

Also in this series:

CHANGE YOUR MIND: 57 WAYS TO UNLOCK YOUR CREATIVE SELF

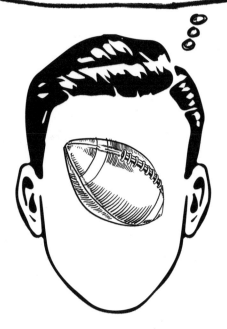

Think Like an Athlete

57 WAYS TO ACHIEVE
YOUR LIFE GOALS

DAVID NICHOLSON

hardie grant books

Every great
athlete
started out
with a

DREAM...

...of emulating their heroes,

...bestriding the tape,

...setting the world alight with their achievements.

The example they set for everyone is simple:

Pursue your goals, live the dream

and...

1. LIVE OUT . . .

YOUR DREAM

WE ALL HAVE DREAMS. BUT IN ORDER TO MAKE DREAMS COME INTO REALITY, IT TAKES AN AWFUL LOT OF DETERMINATION, DEDICATION, SELF-DISCIPLINE AND EFFORT.

Jesse Owens
(100 metres gold medal winner
at the 1936 Berlin Olympics)

As a child, who were your heroes? Footballers? Cricketers? Swimmers? Athletes?

You probably felt that their achievements and performances were somehow superhuman, unattainable, extraordinary. To emulate them would be an impossible dream.

But, just like you, they once dreamed of following their own heroes. And, in most cases, the realisation of those dreams only took place after many years of practice, hard work, disappointments and determination.

Sporting excellence is a fantastic model for anyone to work towards and emulate because it's possible for absolutely anyone to achieve, in their own way.

If you run a kilometre in 10 minutes today, then run it in 9 minutes 50 seconds tomorrow; you are following the example of Sebastian Coe, Mo Farah and every other runner who ever lived. They all dreamed of reaching the line quicker tomorrow.

Equally, dreaming of achievement in your work, in your personal life or in any other field of human endeavour is always positive. It gives you the strength and imagination to become someone different, someone like the heroes you have admired since childhood.

Sporting success can play an instructive role because it is so visible, measurable and widely celebrated. A team wins a cup, an athlete wins a medal.

In your own personal field of achievement there may not be cups and medals awarded, but you will know when you've reached your destination. Because it will feel like a dream come true.

2. TELL YOURSELF SOMETHING OFTEN

There is great power in repetition. Here are five reasons why:

- It fixes something into our memory which makes it easier to achieve in future.

- We can experiment by changing minor things each time until we find exactly the right way to think about something.

- The act of repetition has a ritualistic, rhythmic power, like a chant.

- Words change their meaning when repeated and become more like objects.

- The more we repeat things, the more like a personal mantra they become.

Sportspeople – especially endurance athletes – will often adopt a particular phrase which they repeat as they're performing to help them overcome the pain and exhaustion they feel and to spur them on.

One professional triathlete says to himself: 'Strong legs, strong lungs, strong will' as he cycles 180 km during an Ironman race, and as he pushes through the marathon run at the end.

This 'mind over body' approach to repetition applies in all kinds of ways. It strengthens our determination to overcome obstacles, to rid ourselves of distractions and to commit ourselves to achieving goals.

Every time we repeat something like 'I will get to the end of this' the act of saying it replaces the alternative, which could be 'I'm worried about failing' or 'I'm too tired'.

It's amazing how susceptible the human mind can be to these small tricks, really!

Like the children in *The Sound of Music* – 'I simply remember my favourite things, and then I don't feel so bad!'

Among the many tools in the athlete's mental drawer, repetition is a very useful and powerful one.

> ## IT'S THE REPETITION OF AFFIRMATIONS THAT LEADS TO BELIEF. AND ONCE THAT BELIEF BECOMES A DEEP CONVICTION, THINGS BEGIN TO HAPPEN.

Muhammad Ali
(the greatest boxer in history)

3. FOCUS

ON WHAT *YOU* WANT TO ACHIEVE

If you think about focus from an optical point of view, there are a few important things to consider: is your ambition to realise a full picture, with the entire landscape in focus, together with people and other objects (houses, cars maybe), also in focus? Or does your ideal picture have a specific image at its centre, in sharp focus, with the background less distinct?

For a photographer, the difference is known as 'depth of field'. For an athlete, the difference can be related to personal and team performance. Some sportspeople have distinctly personal goals, related to their own time for an event or in winning a specific competition. Others are more team-oriented.

I DON'T FOCUS ON WHAT I'M UP AGAINST. I FOCUS ON MY GOALS AND I TRY TO IGNORE THE REST.

Venus Williams
(tennis player with
22 Grand Slam titles)

The same applies in life. Perhaps the health and strength of your family is more important to you than your own individual success. Or being part of a thriving business will bring you a greater sense of achievement than boosting your own personal income.

Here are four things that sportspeople consider:

1. For team players, how to tailor their efforts to bring out the best in other people. This may involve shifting their role, so that it becomes more complementary with someone else, rather than highlighting their own exceptional performance. A footballer, for example, will experience deep satisfaction from crossing a ball and watching a teammate score a phenomenal goal.

2. Demonstrating hard work. If we are aware that other people are working hard on our behalf it inspires us to do the same. It sharpens our focus on a joint goal.

3. For individual sportspeople, focusing on a goal will often mean forfeiting something. For example social events, alcohol and late nights.

4. It may also include hours of solitary practice and training, which can place a burden on other people (such as their family). Make sure you take this into account.

All of these issues apply to achieving life goals, just as much as sporting ones. So keep your ideal picture in mind and remember to focus!

4. ADOPT A

In some sports, the 'goal' is simple to spot. It's a big (or not so big) net at the end of the pitch. In others, the goal is much harder to define. Does a team achieve its goal by winning the league, beating its closest rival or simply avoiding relegation?

In everyday life, our goals frequently shift and change shape. Achieving promotion may seem like a worthwhile target, but if the company is threatened with collapse, then everything takes on a different aspect.

Nevertheless, clarity of vision is crucially important.

It means that whatever problems you run up against will seem relatively minor, compared to the rewards offered by the bigger picture. It means that you will be able to guide others (even if they're not intimately involved in your mission) in how they can further

CLEAR VISION

your goals. And it means that you can get out of bed each day with something definable and inspiring to motivate you.

For an athlete, this may be something as remote as the Olympic Games several years away, when they calculate that they will have reached a physical peak, with a certain amount of training under their belt, and several 'practice' events in between.

For the rest of us, this could be the achievement of buying a house, getting married, starting a family or getting a new job. In each case, adopting a clear vision will make these goals all the more realistic and achievable.

> **VISION IS THE ART OF SEEING WHAT IS INVISIBLE TO OTHERS.**
>
> Jonathan Swift
> (author of *Gulliver's Travels*)

Just as athletes can develop 'muscle memory', where the repetition of a physical act becomes automatic, thus easier to achieve, the same applies to our mental abilities. The mind is tremendously adept at creating short cuts and grasping concepts: once it has travelled in a certain direction, whether finding the route from home to work, or navigating a new piece of software, it will guide us back through the maze quicker than before.

To succeed in sport, as in life, it is important both to understand this process and to capitalise on it. Athletes condition their minds to maximise their performance at key moments: the start of a race, the sprint finish, or the uphill section of a cycle course.

In life, there are many similar points of potential stress or decision-making which can be predicted in advance. Are you prepared for the annual review meeting with your boss – have you thought of some points to raise? How about your daughter's wedding – have you prepared a speech?

It's amazing how often people fail to plan for these big occasions, despite having time to prepare in advance. It's not just about constant, repetitive practice, but about the quality of the plans we make. So look at the way athletes prepare for their big events; read the great sporting biographies, detailing the mental preparation of champions, as they approached the huge events of their career.

Mental preparation allows us to become more comfortable with ideas and prospective events which once scared us, or which we thought were out of our reach. Tell yourself you can do it. That's half the battle.

PRACTICE PUTS BRAINS IN YOUR MUSCLES.

Sam Snead
(winner of an all-time-record 82 Professional Golf Association events)

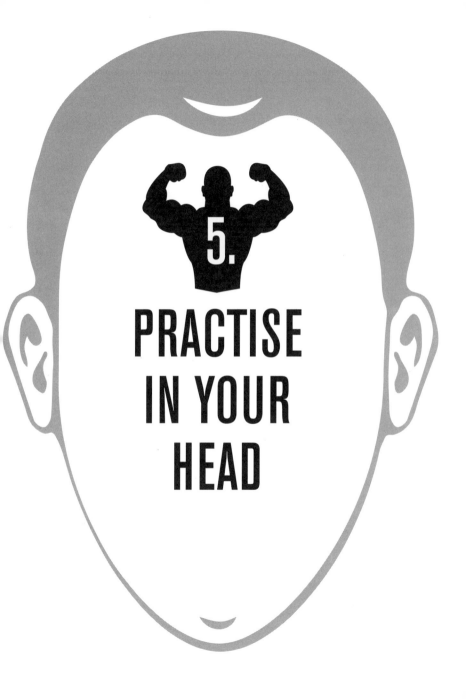

5.

PRACTISE
IN YOUR
HEAD

6. SET SMALL DAILY GOALS

ALS

> **MARGINAL GAINS IS ABOUT MORE THAN PURE TECHNOLOGY. IT IS ABOUT NUTRITION, ERGONOMICS, PSYCHOLOGY. IT IS ABOUT MAKING SURE THE RIDERS GET A GOOD NIGHT'S SLEEP BY TRANSPORTING THEIR OWN BED AND PILLOW TO EACH HOTEL. EACH IMPROVEMENT MAY SEEM TRIVIAL, BUT THE CUMULATIVE EFFECT CAN BE HUGE.**
>
> Sir Dave Brailsford
> (director of UK Cycling)

One of the most astonishing sporting achievements in the past decade has been the performance of the British cycling team, across all its various disciplines, from the velodrome conquests of Sir Chris Hoy and Victoria Pendleton and their colleagues to the Tour de France triumphs of Sir Bradley Wiggins and Chris Froome.

Before 2000, there were barely ever any British cycling achievements of note. So what was different?

By common consent, it has been the work of Sir Dave Brailsford, director of UK cycling. His philosophy can be summarised as 'Do a hundred things one per cent better'. It's also known as 'the aggregation of marginal gains'. To apply the lessons from his sporting approach to real life situations, you have to decide on your goal in life and then work backwards, until you can define the hundred (or at least several dozen) things that will contribute to achieving this goal, if you improve them.

Examples will be:

 Diet: concentrate on tailoring what you eat to realising your ambitions. There is almost always a strong correlation.

 Time management: using your available time in the best way will always improve results.

 Measuring your performance: this may be easier to do in sports than in some areas of life, but if you can spend 10 minutes more per day on something you want to improve, you'll see the difference.

 Building training or practice into your daily routine: the British cycling team's achievements, based on this sporting philosophy, have been phenomenal. It does mean adopting a new and encompassing mentality, but just look at the results!

> **I HAVE BEEN STRUCK AGAIN AND AGAIN BY HOW IMPORTANT MEASUREMENT IS TO IMPROVING THE HUMAN CONDITION.**
>
> Bill Gates
> (founder of Microsoft and one of the world's wealthiest people)

New technology has meant that it is now far easier to measure performance across all kinds of fields than in the past.

Today, we routinely measure our running speed, distance and calories burned, our cycling, swimming and skiing details, meaning that we can track progress in all kinds of unforeseen ways.

It's part of the Big Data revolution, where we have access to a million new pieces of information that were previously impossible to collect.

In sport, there are multiple advantages to these new capabilities. Instead of running, swimming or cycling 'blind', not knowing our speed or distance, we're more able to pace ourselves and judge our performance against previous efforts and against our peers. Using technology such as GPS and systems like Strava we can compare our efforts with those of both friends and complete strangers.

7. MAKE YOUR GOAL

In non-sporting life, the same applies. We can count calories through inputting what we've eaten into online programmes, which calculate the total and show us whether we're on target.

We can measure our financial situation in far greater detail than before, with automatic programmes stripping out amounts paid for work expenses, loan repayments, savings and investments, for example.

And our computers have become individual repositories of a vast trove of valuable information, with all of our thousands of emails, documents and online histories stored away.

Sportspeople are pioneers in using data to improve their performance and spur their motivation: instead of becoming demotivated when they're out running, they can draw comfort from statistics. 'That's another 10 km I've run today, making 60 km this week', they say, rather than bemoaning a slow time.

Technology is our friend. Don't be afraid to use it.

MEASURABLE IMPROVEMENT

To make serious progress, you need to tread a path between extending yourself – which (in sporting terms) improves your strength, skills and stamina – and demanding so much that you fail badly and lose interest. So pitching your intermediate goals is extremely important.

An athlete will have a carefully calibrated series of goals to achieve in the months, even years, leading up to a major event. For a runner, this could include:

· 'Fun runs' in a local park, where the results aren't important and the atmosphere is casual, but there are a handful of talented and quick runners. In some places, these take place once a week, so it's easy to check your progress and to get mildly challenging race practice.

· Cross-country competitions. These are likely to involve mud, hills and even water hazards (depending on the weather), and so offer a stiffer challenge to all runners. Top athletes, such as Mo Farah and Sally Pearson, spent much of their youth competing in these events before concentrating on the truly elite races.

· Training camps, where you live alongside athletes of a similar (or higher) ability, so that you can stretch yourself and try to match their effort and attainment.

8. SET CHALLENGING BUT

The equivalent in non-sporting terms – for an artist for example – could be:

· Exhibiting work in the local library, or similar public space, alongside other local artists.

· Submitting your work for regional art fairs.

· Taking a residential course to study with artists and talented amateurs to improve technique and composition.

You want to be encouraged by your results, without becoming complacent. And if you do crash and burn, then take a step back, recalibrate and try again.

> SUCCESS IS DUE TO OUR STRETCHING TO THE CHALLENGES OF LIFE. FAILURE COMES WHEN WE SHRINK FROM THEM.

John C. Maxwell
(leadership author)

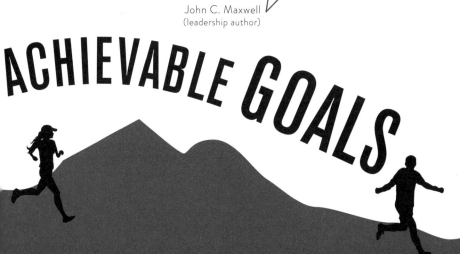

ACHIEVABLE GOALS

9.
ACKNOWLEDGE ALL YOUR EFFORTS

Everyone needs encouragement but, unlike children, most people don't have someone nearby who will offer praise and encouragement for all the little things we do. (Even in the most loving marriage, there are limits to the amount of support that each can offer the other.) So it's down to us to play that role for ourselves.

There is an element of split personality here. You have to imagine that one side of your psyche is complimenting the other, reinforcing the notion that – as a whole person – you're making good progress and achieving your goals.

Here are some suggested ways to do this:

- Think of how you were before you took action to realise your goals. For example, the 'you' that weighed more, that hadn't gained a new skill, that was still blocked by some obstacle.

- Think of this person praising the new 'you' on these achievements, almost in astonishment that they have happened at all!

- Use different ways to record your achievements, whether getting pictures of yourself in action, or at a particular place, or noting down your progress.

- Remember that 'progress' and 'efforts' can mean what you want them to mean. Persistence is one form of progress, which has few outwards signs but is nevertheless vital.

How you feel about changes in your life is, in the end, more important than the hard evidence that is visible to the world.

The vast majority of sportspeople will never win a major event, perform in front of a big crowd, or share a stage with international athletes.

What matters to them is that they have beaten their own expectations, realised their own personal goals and had a lot of enjoyment and fun along the way – and they've improved their health.

This is true for many other areas of life.

THE REWARD OF A WORK IS TO HAVE PRODUCED IT; THE REWARD OF EFFORT IS TO HAVE GROWN BY IT.

Antonin Sertillanges
(philosopher)

10.

THINK POSITIVELY

> # WE CAN COMPLAIN BECAUSE ROSE BUSHES HAVE THORNS, OR REJOICE BECAUSE THORN BUSHES HAVE ROSES.

Abraham Lincoln
(16th president of
the United States)

The medical benefits of positive thinking are well established: lower blood pressure, less incidence of conditions such as stomach ulcers and general stress-related illnesses, and many more. But ordering yourself to think positively is seldom going to be enough. Blind optimism is no substitute for a constructive, well-balanced positive outlook on life and on the future.

Where athletes have a natural advantage in this field is in their biological make-up. Exercise produces endorphins, which interact with receptors in the brain, meaning that you feel less pain. These chemicals are manufactured in your brain, spinal cord and elsewhere, leading to reduced stress and anxiety, higher self-esteem and improved sleep. They also make you feel more energised and positive about life. This makes exercise a wonderfully self-reinforcing activity: the more you do it, the better you feel, and the better you feel, the higher your achievements are likely to go.

There are few other kinds of activity which have this level of self-reinforcing, virtuous circle to them, but here are some disciplines where there are parallels:

- When learning a new language you become immersed in that culture, history and society, reinforcing your understanding of its vocabulary and grammar, but also coming to love its people.

- Team activities outside working hours can make you appreciate your colleagues more; work life can improve as you develop a sense of loyalty to the business and gain satisfaction from teamwork.

- In your personal relationships, arguments can be upsetting but try to see them as opportunities to strengthen your bond for the future, just as overcoming injuries can improve an athlete's sporting performance.

11. ENJOY

For the great majority of them, fate has dealt athletes and sportspeople the most amazing, unbelievable hand. They get paid for having fun! For playing games, rolling around on the grass, frolicking in the water or jumping up and down with a ball.

All the athletes I've ever met have a kind of inner confidence that is different to arrogance. It's about having a physical gift, recognised by many thousands if not millions of people, which has elevated them to a state of grace. They are blessed. As a result, it's almost impossible for them not to have fun and enjoy themselves.

You can see the same thing with artists, musicians, writers and many other professionals who love what they do with a great intensity and are hugely thankful that the world values their abilities sufficiently to reward them for doing what they love to do anyway.

Everyone can tap into this feeling if they set their minds to it. People's activities — whether paid or unpaid — are unique to them and they're able to carry them out thanks to a combination of experience, natural attributes and circumstances.

YOURSELF

So the trick is to love what you do and thank your stars (or your God) for giving you the chance to do what you do, to be where you are and to use whatever gift you have.

Seize the opportunities, think like an athlete and enjoy your work, social life and sport to their fullest extents.

> ## WITHOUT THE ELEMENT OF ENJOYMENT, IT IS NOT WORTH TRYING TO EXCEL AT ANYTHING.

Magnus Carlsen
(reigning World Chess Champion)

12. MASTER SELF-CONTROL

Whether on the track or in the field, a team game or an individual event, excelling at sport centres around self-control: you have to control your body, your mind and your emotions. You need to urge your limbs on to do your bidding and persevere where the automatic response would be to stop and rest. In some cases, the sheer length of a competitive event is unimaginable for most non-athletes. For instance, an Ironman triathlon will typically last between 8–10 hours.

How do athletes develop this self-control and apply it to their sports? Firstly, there is an absolute focus on a goal, which means tailoring your activities and training to that end. Then it's about adopting good habits, which reinforce those activities, such as early nights and early mornings, good nutrition and staying away from alcohol and cake. And, finally, it's about keeping track of your progress, noting your achievements, visualising your target and maintaining a rigorous focus on your plan.

BY CONSTANT SELF-DISCIPLINE AND SELF-CONTROL YOU CAN DEVELOP GREATNESS OF CHARACTER.

Grenville Kleiser
(Canadian author of inspirational literature)

Maintaining self-control brings all kinds of benefits:

· Greater awareness of our surroundings and of each other.
· More focus on our goals, whether personal, professional or social.
· Less potential for damaging arguments with friends or relations.
· More opportunity to plan ahead and to make good choices in life.

Self-control can be taught, but it is easy to succumb to the temptations of indolence, lust or greed. What we can learn from athletes is how rich the rewards are for maintaining self-control over time. No serious sportsperson can treat their vocation as a 9–5 business, after which they can go off for a pint, a curry and a cigarette. They have to immerse themselves in the discipline necessary to achieve their goals. Similarly, if you want to move to a bigger house, it might well mean putting in longer hours at work and going out less. If something matters to you that much, and you're completely determined to achieve your goal, then take note of how athletes live and behave. Good luck!

13.
STUDY YOUR DISCI-PLINE

Anyone who has watched *A Question of Sport* will appreciate the depth of knowledge that most sportspeople have for their own discipline. They are aware not only of their own generation of great competitors, but the history of their event or discipline going back a century or more.

In these past 150 years, since the development of the modern Olympic Games (1896), the football World Cup (1930), and the other great international sporting fixtures and organisations such as the Tour de France for cycling (1903), the America's Cup for sailing (1851), the Test series in cricket (1877) and the National Basketball Association (1946), there has been a flourishing of sporting activity unprecedented in human history.

And we can see all around us that this evolution and multiplication of our sporting life remains in progress. Tens of thousands more participants join in public races and sports events each year. Our parks are teeming with runners and cyclists, our pools, with swimmers.

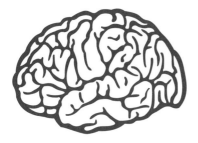

The beauty of this, for an athlete, is that there is so much to study, so much to learn from and so much that can still be achieved. World records continue to tumble with each successive Olympic Games and major event. The speed and skill of professional sportspeople such as footballers (among many others) is breathtaking.

To absorb themselves in their discipline, committed athletes will commonly study the history of their event, the psychological make-up of its great practitioners alongside their biographical details, read tales of heroism and how individuals overcame difficulties and look for tips on training and tactics.

In life we can follow this example by immersing ourselves in projects and taking a similar approach: study those who have excelled at your discipline, how they have reached their position and what their specific attributes or characteristics were. Use the lessons of sports psychology to inspire you when preparing for an interview, setting up a business venture or when sitting an exam.

> # The values learned on the playing field – how to set goals, endure, take criticism and risks, become team players, use our beliefs, stay healthy and deal with stress – prepare us for life.

Donna de Varona
(swimming gold medal winner
in the 1964 Tokyo Olympics)

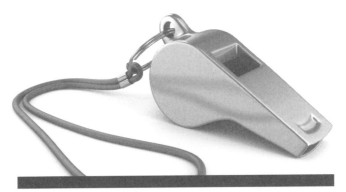

14. LISTEN TO YOUR INNER COACH

Reading biographies of sportsmen and women is an excellent way to feed and develop your inner coach. Although personal trainers for both sport and general life issues are becoming more common, most of us cannot afford the time or money to hire one. So spending some money on a paperback can be a great investment.

The best I've ever come across is *Open*, by tennis player Andre Agassi. His accounts of his training regime, how he would practise for hours in his backyard in Las Vegas, how he would sprint up hills to improve his conditioning and work on his opponents' psychologies, is a gripping read and inspires you to go out and perform at your peak.

Agassi had the foresight to hire a ghostwriter – Pulitzer Prize-winning journalist and author J. R. Moehringer. This was Agassi's own literary coach, distilling a highly readable, even thrilling, account of his sporting life from hundreds of hours of tape recordings. But Agassi had built his career on hiring fantastic coaches, as the book explains.

A great coach will pick training routines which achieve particular goals. Of course physical fitness, strength and stamina are important, but so is keeping your interest, staying amused, dealing with specific strengths and weaknesses in your conditioning and preparing for upcoming events.

In the same way, you can become your own coach by devising a routine which covers these issues, applied to your own life. We all need to keep our skills honed, our reactions sharp, our stamina for lengthy tests intact. But it's also important to keep our diet of activities varied – for our amusement, to correct weaknesses and to reinforce strengths.

At least, that's what we should do, and what a coach would get us to do. Left to our own devices, we typically take the easy path and do the same as last time. That's why we need to listen to our inner coach (and build them up, so they're strong enough to tell us what to do). A strong inner coach will tell us not to skip our evening language class for a night at the pub, for instance.

> EVEN IF IT'S NOT YOUR IDEAL LIFE, YOU CAN ALWAYS CHOOSE IT. NO MATTER WHAT YOUR LIFE IS, CHOOSING IT CHANGES EVERYTHING.

Andre Agassi
(tennis player and multiple Grand Slam winner)

It's commonly said of great athletes that they appear to have more time than anyone else. As though time itself slows down as the ball approaches their bat, racquet or boot. This may somehow be true: just as some people can run more quickly than others, the best ball players can compute the physical coordinates of a moving object at greater speed, allowing them a wealth of options in how, where and with what power to strike it. There must be few other explanations for the way that the world's greatest ball players are able to rise so far above the mass of humanity in their control and mastery of their sport. To an extent, this ability comes from constant practice and dedication. It also comes from a pin-sharp focus on the moment, to the exclusion of all distractions.

Such intense focus has become harder to achieve in the digital age. Even at dinner with our closest friends, many of us resort to checking our emails and Facebook status, something that had no equivalent in pre-smartphone days. At work and at leisure there are similar distractions, as omnipresent connectivity reduces us to bleeping, vibrating, tweeting aerials for each other's needy messaging.

Even marathon runners are now plagued by this desperation to communicate at all times. 'I'm just running over Tower Bridge,' panted one competitor on his phone to his wife, when I took part in the London event.

Take note of the concentration and single-mindedness of professional athletes and give yourself over to the moment. You'll enjoy sport, work and play all the more if you focus on each at the right time and allow them to work their magic.

LACK OF DIRECTION, NOT LACK OF TIME, IS THE PROBLEM. WE ALL HAVE 24-HOUR DAYS.

Zig Ziglar
(motivational speaker and author)

15.
FOCUS
ON
THE
MOMENT

16.
WRITE IT DOWN

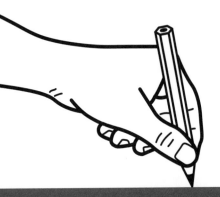

Putting pen to paper (or keystrokes
to computer) and stating your goal
is a physical act. It takes almost no
physical energy, but it casts a powerful
psychological spell. You've made a
decision. You've created a permanent
(or at least lasting) reminder of that
decision and it will stay there until you've
achieved the ambition you've described.
Or else the time that goes by, since you
wrote it, will grow heavier: it will be more annoying in a way.
'Why have you taken so long to do this?'

> **I WRITE TO UNDERSTAND, AS MUCH AS TO BE UNDERSTOOD.**
>
> Elie Wiesel
> (author and winner
> of the Nobel Peace Prize)

An athlete will write down the times they want to achieve, the
distances they want to cover, the drills to perform and the events to
enter. These notes are a form of self-discipline, like the psyche telling
itself what to do.

We all have our active, energetic, purposeful sides as well as our lazy,
easily distracted sides. Writing down goals and targets is a way for the
active side to get the better of the lazy side.

You can choose whether this written record is public or private. Some
people pin their ambitions to the wall for all to see – a weight-loss
chart for example, or a fundraising ladder. This can help achieve extra
motivation, from a combination of positive encouragement and the
fear of criticism following failure or delay.

Most of us keep our notes well away from others. But they're still
mighty helpful.

17. GET OVER THE

HOW?

'Impossible is nothing' goes the Adidas slogan, with a strong nod in the direction of sporting superstars who have made the seemingly impossible appear to be the most natural thing in the world.

Sporting achievement is often like that. If you or I tried running 100 metres, we would do well to finish in much under 15 seconds. By that time, the great sprinters would already be halfway round the next bend. The best marathon runners finish their events and have had time for lunch and a midday nap before the rest of us plod home.

Even so, hundreds of thousands of people do complete marathons each year. Perhaps millions worldwide. The daunting prospect of covering 26 miles – more than most people would ever consider running, for any reason – becomes a wonderfully satisfying achievement.

Many of life's great challenges can be overcome with a similar mindset. Setting up your own business venture, for example. Taking it step-by-step and doing research is the place to start. Marathon runners get over the initial obstacle of 'how can I do it?' by looking at the thousands of others who have done it and asking 'why not?' Similarly, anyone thinking of starting their own business can take heart from the many thousands of others who have set up on their own.

The specific inspiration of professional sport, though, is how it appears to catapult people through a superhuman force field and into another dimension. When you begin to take sport more seriously as an amateur, you retain this sense of awe about the top-level athletes, but you start to approach – quite slowly and cautiously – something closer to their spirit. You detect the amount of

The difference between impossible and possible lies in a person's determination.

Tommy Lasorda
(legendary baseball pitcher and manager of the Dodgers)

dedication and perseverance they have invested in their discipline, the tight focus on achievement and success.

Armed with this knowledge, so much more in life becomes possible. You understand more about stamina, about overcoming pain, about the rewards that come from patient endeavour.

IT IS NO LONGER ABOUT THE 'HOW'

BUT ABOUT
'WHEN'

You know that the end result is within reach and you're biding your time until it comes.

Endurance sports are booming. Millions of competitors throng the world's marathon events from Toronto to Tokyo. Triathlons now attract those middle-aged men and women for whom golf was the previous sport of choice. Swimmers plough from island to island, or flush down the course of mighty rivers. The trend has emerged as the benefits of strenuous exercise have become more widely known, as obesity has become an international epidemic and as an ageing (but still healthy) population looks for new sporting challenges.

With the rise of endurance sports has come new opportunities for participants to learn from their sporting experiences. To improve as a cyclist, for example, you have no other choice but to spend hours upon hours in the saddle, conditioning your body (principally the legs, but the arms and core need to be strong too). Personally, I've spent more than 60 hours in the past month riding more than 1,000 km up mountains in the French Alps and hills all over Yorkshire, following the route of the Tour de France.

I feel a new sense of endurance after all this effort. I feel that I could take part in a long, gruelling, tough and sapping competition lasting anything up to eight hours, and I'd be fine. This is just as well, since I'm just about to enter a half-Ironman triathlon, which includes a swim in the freezing North Sea.

18. PRACTISE

Meanwhile, this training has also equipped me to handle other kinds of endurance. Sitting through long work presentations or wedding services, watching long and slow-moving films, taking long train or car journeys around the country. These can all be testing in their different ways, but the acquisition of sporting endurance has made them not only more bearable but curiously pleasurable. I have new reserves of patience and strength, a kind of mental stamina which was less developed before.

So I'd thoroughly recommend spending up to 8 hours a day in the saddle – find the most attractive scenery possible and a bunch of good companions, set your computer watch to 'start' and off you go.

ENDURANCE

THE FIRST VIRTUE IN A SOLDIER IS ENDURANCE OF FATIGUE; COURAGE IS ONLY THE SECOND VIRTUE.

Napoleon Bonaparte
(French emperor and general)

Staying strong is subtly different to having great endurance – which is mainly about physical stamina – or mental toughness. It's about conditioning your body and mind to perform at its peak when you most need it. For an athlete, it's those parts of a race where the competition is fiercest: where the cycle route starts up a steep hill or, for a runner, when another competitor tries to break away. In life it's often about picking yourself up after failure – being passed over for promotion, perhaps. How can you learn from the experience, move on and achieve your goal after all?

You can achieve this kind of deep physical strength through training patterns. A good coach will get you to spend time on arduous basic exercises to wear you down, then make you sprint up a hill, for example. This will condition your muscles to respond in a new way to the demands of a race situation.

When the time comes, you will find you have another gear (to use a motoring metaphor) to call upon, which you never knew you had.

To draw a parallel in business and social life, think of the ways in which you've had to struggle to overcome obstacles. The exams you were worried about passing. The interviews which made you anxious. The times in life when you failed and had to try again.

These are the reservoirs of strength in your character which you can call upon at times of difficulty. Like physical strength, created by stressing your body, mental strength is created in a similar way. Once you recognise this, you're more able to draw upon it at will.

By both practising the physical exercises that make you stronger and more able to respond at moments of crisis, and understanding the mental equivalents that you've developed over time, you'll be better equipped to achieve your goals, whatever they are.

19. STAY
STRONG

THE RESISTANCE THAT YOU FIGHT PHYSICALLY IN
THE GYM AND THE RESISTANCE THAT YOU FIGHT IN
LIFE CAN ONLY BUILD A STRONG CHARACTER.

Arnold Schwarzenegger
(bodybuilder, actor and politician)

20. CHOOSE ACTIVITIES THAT MAKE YOU FEEL POWERFUL

Reaching athletic goals is a long-term, careful process. Athletes need to prepare for important events that may be some years ahead, building their performances and capabilities up gradually, week by week, month by month.

To help them in this journey, they will set particular goals which, although testing, are certainly achievable. Reaching these goals reassures them that they're on the right path, that they're making the right progress. In sport and in life it brings a sense of fulfilment and power just to say that you've made it.

Here are some examples:

• Reach a good weight for your event. NB: Experts advise that you shouldn't lose more than 2 lb (just under 1 kg) per week.

• Finish a race in a new personal best time. If you're a runner, you can make this more likely by choosing a flat course (and by training on a hilly course).

• Complete a training camp in a related discipline. Cyclists can improve their conditioning by spending time running, and vice versa. Footballers can improve their conditioning by swimming.

• Spend time coaching young athletes. They will benefit from your experience and you'll feel stronger by comparison with them.

Equally, personal and business progress can be enhanced by choosing your activities carefully.

For example:

- Keep your weight down. The more weight the rest of society puts on, the more you will stand out (and improve your health) if you have a good Body Mass Index (BMI).

- Take on a challenge that's related to your work or hobbies, but more testing than you've done before. Study for a qualification, perhaps, or enter a competition.

- Do something new that will be complementary to your goals, such as volunteering to go to a work-related conference abroad.

- Spend time passing on your skills and experience to young people.

KNOWLEDGE IS POWER.

Sir Francis Bacon
(philosopher and statesman)

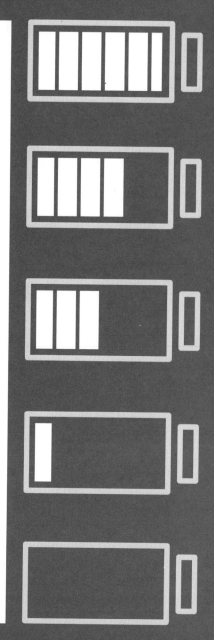

21. BE FLEXIBLE

Have you ever watched a gymnast and wondered how on earth they can get their body to reach such extraordinary positions? Legs doing the splits, back arched so far that their head is between their thighs?

Gymnasts certainly spend many years developing this kind of flexibility, but that doesn't mean they were born with a special kind of body. Almost all of us could have achieved the same level of bendiness, had we trained for the same amount of time, with the same dedication.

Muscles, tendons, joints and limbs are all capable of stretching and bending way more than the routine postures that we hold in everyday life. It simply takes practice and training, ideally with a good coach who knows how the body works and can provide helpful exercises.

In the same way, what we achieve in our own lives can mirror the enhanced flexibility that athletes routinely expect.

"STAY COMMITTED TO YOUR DECISIONS, BUT STAY FLEXIBLE IN YOUR APPROACH."

Tony Robbins (motivational speaker and author)

Here are some exercises and ideas that could help to improve your general flexibility:

· Study a foreign language. Appreciating the way another language works will increase your mental flexibility and dexterity.

· Make a point of talking to someone new at parties. It will take you out of your comfort zone, in a positive way.

· Take the stairs instead of the lift. Cycle to work instead of driving. Bake your own bread.

· Spend time camping and walking in the wilderness. Being close to nature will remind you how flexible humans have had to be, to survive for so long.

22.

DESIGN A TAILORED PROGRAMME

Whenever a budding athlete or sportsperson is spotted by a knowledgeable scout – maybe the coach of a local sports team, or a fellow athlete – they are thrust into a new training programme. Whatever they were doing beforehand was probably wrong, or at least not sufficient. They need to learn new techniques, new training methods, adjust their diet and start focusing more on dates far into the future.

If you are serious about achieving your life goals, then this should be your approach too. Imagine that someone has spotted you and marked you out for future success. This 'someone' can be yourself. Why not? You have earmarked yourself to do well. So now go ahead and devise a tailored training programme for yourself, whether it's designed for you to lose weight, learn a new skill, get a qualification or land a new job. It may involve hiring a coach, because that will give you the benefit of professional advice and experience. But it may not.

Here is a suggested checklist for your programme, so adapt it to fit your circumstances:

- Write down your goals.
- Decide on a schedule to achieve them.
- Join a group of like-minded people local to you (if appropriate).
- Read up on your subject, whether through biographies of celebrated people who have done what you're aiming to do, or histories of the field.
- Spend a few hours each week on your chosen activity, measuring your results.
- Share your results with a friend or colleague and discuss ways to improve.
- Reward yourself for achievements, however modest.

And, most importantly of all, make a start. Get up off your backside and do it! There's no turning back.

23. APPLY PROVEN

TRAINING METHODS

For an addict, the first step towards recovery is admitting that they have a problem. For anyone looking to achieve challenging goals, it can be a similar moment of clarity and recognition that leads to progress. They realise they need help!

This is completely routine for athletes, who seldom approach competitive events without a professional coach to devise a detailed training schedule and programme. For everyone else, it's a bigger step. You may feel your money can be better spent in other ways. You may find it hard to put aside the time to train or to work out how you're going to achieve your goals in life. Yet the commitment – both in money and time – is very likely to pay dividends.

An almost alchemic reaction takes place when an athlete meets their ideal coach: the athlete becomes more motivated, the coach is inspired to guide them towards greater achievements and together they go on to do wonders.

In life, we value things that cost us. A freebie is great, but its value is diminished because we have expended neither effort nor time to get it.

Once you've taken the step of taking on a coach, or simply adopting a training programme, then the hard work begins.

Whether for sport or in life, there are a number of training principles:

· Keep your sessions regular and predictable. Your body and mind should grow to expect a weekly (or daily, or whatever) training session. This will help you get the most from each session and improve your satisfaction levels.

· Work to a high intensity throughout the sessions. It's not about simply covering old ground, it's about extending your capabilities and developing your physical and/or mental muscles. It should be intense and challenging.

· Vary the sessions. This is a proven technique to keep training interesting and to ensure that your various muscle groups (or mental faculties) are all kept sharp and fit. So in physical training, variety means a combination of short, sharp exercises and longer ones; some that give you a cardiovascular workout (good for burning fat) and others that are more aerobic – longer distance runs, cycles or swims.

In non-sporting terms, this perhaps means varying between more mentally intense exercises such as sudoku and opera and more reflective exercises such as reading novels or gardening.

> ## IT'S ALL TO DO WITH THE TRAINING. YOU CAN DO A LOT IF YOU'RE PROPERLY TRAINED.

Queen Elizabeth II
(monarch, racehorse- and dog-owner,
grandmother of an Olympic medal winner)

STRIVE FOR BALANCE IN LIFE. BE SINGLE-MINDED WHEN IT COMES TO YOUR GOALS, BUT DON'T LET EVERYTHING IN YOUR LIFE GET

OUT OF KILTER

24. Seek out the BEST advice

To reach their full potential, almost all athletes need a coach or trainer with the experience to guide their training, monitor their progress and encourage them to push on to greater things.

This will help them to set goals, analyse their performance, provide advice and suggestions for training methods and technique, and discuss tactics for future games, races or events.

The key factors that contribute to a good athlete–coach relationship include:

• A good personality fit between the two sides. Both should respect and like one another so that they become a team with common ambitions and goals.

- An experienced coach who can draw upon lessons from working with other athletes (or indeed having been an athlete) so that they can give you a helpful perspective.

- A coach with a strong background in sports science. This is an excellent asset, because they can explain the reasoning behind various training methods and how they are beneficial.

- The athlete is a good listener. This is crucial to take advantage of the advice given and put it into practice.

The rise of 'life coaches' demonstrates how many non-athletes are already adopting the approach to improving skills and conditioning that athletes have long understood.

It applies in our work life, where experienced business mentors can provide excellent help and advice, and our personal life, through hiring experts in almost anything that interests us (gardening, travel or music). The digital age has made this evermore straightforward and possible, allowing mentoring and coaching to take place across continents, using video and other online communication.

Recently I met a US-based professional cyclist and Ironman triathlete who coaches a British triathlete, sending him training routines and advice every few days, then meeting up a couple of times a year. It was a strong and highly effective relationship, despite the long distances involved.

I THINK THAT'S THE SINGLE BEST PIECE OF ADVICE: CONSTANTLY THINK ABOUT HOW YOU COULD BE DOING THINGS BETTER AND QUESTIONING YOURSELF.

Elon Musk
(co-founder of PayPal,
Tesla Motors and SpaceX)

25. SHARE YOUR GOALS AND DRAW MOTIVATION

People are naturally gregarious. They perform well in teams and in public, they respond well to encouragement, they excel when presented with competition. Although many athletes have to train alone, simply because there is no option, they recognise that group sessions can yield exceptional benefits. Runners make the biggest leaps in their performance when they attend group track sessions, sprinting round an athletics track in repetitions of 400, 800 or 1,200 metres, all in a pack and trying to outrun one another. The same applies in most other sports.

Over time, this joint encouragement through working with fellow athletes becomes a virtuous circle of encouragement, support when things aren't going so well, social interaction and positive competitive rivalry. Joint ambitions are hatched, goals identified; people gain higher confidence from one another and the whole becomes greater than the sum of the parts.

This almost magical transformation in an athlete's performance levels can transfer into all kinds of other fields, if wisely followed. In business, for example:

· Seek out people who share your interests and ambitions at a similar level.

· Share your concerns and queries, your hopes and fears. Finding someone who is going through similar experiences can be tremendously reassuring and helpful.

· Learn from people who have encountered obstacles along the way and overcome them.

· Try to capture that spirit of communal achievement which a sporting group can engender – the camaraderie, the sense of competing with one another in a positive sense.

There are, of course, substantial differences between sport and business, but finding a mentor in the workplace can be invaluable for helping determine and achieve career goals. And although many workplaces promote an ethos of collaboration, healthy competition can often spur colleagues on; everyone aiming to create the best possible product, for example.

> **WHATEVER WE POSSESS BECOMES OF DOUBLE VALUE WHEN WE CAN SHARE IT WITH OTHERS.**
>
> Jean-Nicolas Bouilly (writer and politician)

THE ONLY REASON FOR TIME IS SO THAT EVERYTHING DOESN'T HAPPEN AT ONCE.
Albert Einstein (theoretical physicist)

26. MANAGE YOUR TIME WISELY

The human body and the human mind have similar parameters. Athletes train for a certain number of hours a day because that works best. They don't spend 12 hours a day flat out. In the same way, we've evolved to spend around 8 hours a day working, because that suits our energies and attention span. But athletes have to be more shrewd about their use of time than simply allotting a certain number of hours to the task.

For a swimmer, for example, a typical day might look like this:

6.00 a.m.   Two-hour training session including drills with fins and pull buoys (to exercise particular muscles).
8.00 a.m.   One-hour weight-training in the gym, with flexibility workout.
9.00 a.m.   Breakfast of protein and carbohydrate, then back to bed for 2 hours' rest.
1.00 p.m.   Lunch of grilled chicken and salad.
3.00 p.m.   Land session to build flexibility and core strength.
5.00 p.m.   Second 2-hour pool session with different drills and sets to stress one or more of the energy systems.

Each session is designed to strengthen different muscles or to develop certain aspects of fitness, strength or stamina, while minimising the risk of injury. And then, when an event is close, training diminishes as the athlete 'tapers' – to ensure that they're at maximum freshness and full of energy for the day itself.

Adopting a similar approach can be very helpful for anyone committed to pursuing their goals. It means allowing time for rest, varying the routine, but nevertheless maintaining an intensity and dedication to achieving the optimal result. So perhaps if you're setting up a business this might mean making time to see potential business contacts in the evening, but also leaving enough time for yourself to exercise and spend time with friends and family. Balance is all.

27. MANAGE YOUR

EXPECTATIONS

Even a world-class athlete like Mo Farah, with his multiple Olympic gold medals and international championship victories, has to admit: 'I've lost more races than I've won.'

This is true of almost all athletes. Having a poor race, getting beaten and making mistakes is a major part of sport, as in life. If a meeting at work goes badly, think about what went wrong and why. Managing your expectations is about recognising the value of these low points and then working hard to prevent a repetition.

Sporting literature is full of people talking about 'bouncing back' from defeats and 'never giving up'. These are important attributes, but I prefer to concentrate on what you can learn from a difficult experience.

In the triathlon, for example, competitors will often find that they have one slow leg out of the three, which drags their overall time down. So for the next event, they'll practise extra hard at this discipline in order to solve this problem.

Managing expectations is also about facing your own demons and challenging yourself, rather than the other athletes on the track (or wherever you're competing). If you run the best race you're capable of, the result will take care of itself.

And so in life. People recognise the qualities of someone who is putting their best efforts into their work, trying to fulfil their potential. So your boss gave you that new account to manage and it's not going smoothly. Talk to your boss and client, work out what's going wrong and why and learn from it. People fall short sometimes, particularly if they are ambitious and go for difficult challenges. That's fine as long as you learn from it and move on.

If you're in danger of becoming discouraged – perhaps you've made a mistake at work – just think of Olympic gold medallist Mo Farah, losing a race for the 100th time, but determined to learn from the experience.

"BEING THE BEST YOU CAN BE IS POSSIBLE ONLY IF YOUR **DESIRE** TO BE A CHAMPION IS **GREATER** THAN YOUR FEAR OF FAILURE."

Dr Sammy Lee (Olympic champion diver)

MANAGE YOUR PRIORITIES

28.

When asked on their deathbed what they regret, some people say they wished they'd spent more time with their families. Others say they wish they'd spent less time working. Groucho Marx said he wished he'd tried more positions (in bed).

In a recent survey, the number one regret was: 'I wish I'd had the courage to be true to myself, instead of living the life that others expected of me.'

So to prevent having to say that (if someone is rude enough to ask you on your deathbed), take action now! Have the courage, be true to yourself and set your own priorities.

For many athletes, the decision to be 'true' to themselves and to pursue a sporting goal is the crucial turning point in their lives. Their families may warn that athletes suffer short careers and emerge with few prospects once their competitive time is done. Athletes may

I HAVE ALWAYS TRIED TO BE TRUE TO MYSELF, TO PICK THOSE BATTLES I FELT WERE IMPORTANT. MY ULTIMATE RESPONSIBILITY IS TO MYSELF. I COULD NEVER BE ANYTHING ELSE.

Arthur Ashe
(tennis player and triple
Grand Slam champion)

doubt their abilities and be envious of their peers as they go through their teens and twenties in a haze of debauchery.

But it's their life and they've taken a brave decision to commit themselves to sport, much as someone might commit themselves to becoming an actor or artist. They are all roads paved with risk, but the rewards can be tremendous.

Whatever your goals, you have to ask yourself whether they mean enough to you to forfeit other things. It may be time with your family (that other common deathbed regret). It may be financial security or career progression. It may be something as seemingly marginal as alcohol.

But if you truly want to achieve something big in your life, then it will have to rise up the list of your priorities. And there are few better role models than athletes, who often sacrifice almost all of the other pleasures in life to become the best they can be.

Alongside physical training, nutrition is a key component of sporting success. Top athletes pay a great deal of attention to it and have finely detailed plans of what to eat, how much, and when. The thinking behind their nutrition plan will include:

- A carefully worked-out calorie intake, to match the calorie expenditure of training and performance.
- Choosing foods that enhance conditioning and performance – typically low-fat, high-protein, with carbohydrates at specific times.
- Timing meals at specific intervals. For instance, breakfast is important as it kick-starts the body's metabolism. Also, plenty of protein straight after exercise, when it is most readily absorbed, is beneficial.
- Eating food that will release energy over the required timespan, such as porridge for middle- and long-distance events.
- Using high-sugar gels and isotonic drinks during races to replace salt and provide an extra energy boost.

Well-balanced and carefully thought out nutrition will have a positive effect on anyone, whatever their physical activities or lifestyle. A good BMI of between 18.5 and 25 will help to prevent many illnesses including heart disease and diabetes. Nutrition is central to achieving this. Besides keeping you at the right weight, good nutrition aids concentration, energy, strength and stamina – all helpful attributes in life as well as sport.

Here are some key suggestions for a good nutritional balance:

•••

Choose fresh fruit and vegetables.

•••

Choose white meat (such as chicken) and fish over red or processed meat.

•••

Choose vegetable sauces such as tomato over cream sauces.

•••

Avoid excessive bread or fried foods like chips, ice cream or cakes.

29. PAY ATTENTION TO NUTRITION

YOU MAY BE SURPRISED TO HEAR THAT I DON'T ORDER PIZZA WHEN I GET IN.

Andy Murray (2013 Wimbledon tennis champion)

Knowing what you want is half the battle. Many athletes have figured out the route they want their lives to take by the time they're in school. As a 9 year old, they'll be transfixed by the sight of a swimmer, or a World Cup football match, or a marathon.

That's great fortune, because having that early obsession clears the way for all kinds of blessings. Their muscles can develop in the best way as they train in their chosen discipline. They can learn from their peers at school and in sports clubs, make all their early mistakes and get that adrenalin rush from young victories which will see them through tougher times. These lucky athletes need no reminding to stick to their goals. Their goals are almost part of them.

30. STICK TO

For later developers, the road is harder. Whether in sport or in life, the older you are when you decide to pursue a goal, the more willpower it takes to get there and the more you will feel the sacrifice from giving up competing interests. Whether you've decided to start up your own business, exercise more or eat more healthily, the crucial thing is that when you've set your sights on something, don't be deflected, no matter what the temptation.

YOUR GOALS

Much of this is self-discipline, one of the elements of any successful enterprise. So here are some principles of self-discipline to bear in mind:

- Stick to a routine, so that in time it becomes automatic.

- Surround yourself with people who support your activities rather than distract you.

- Record your progress.

- Keep your eyes on the prize, even when you're feeling overwhelmed.

31. PRACTISE MENTAL TOUGHNESS

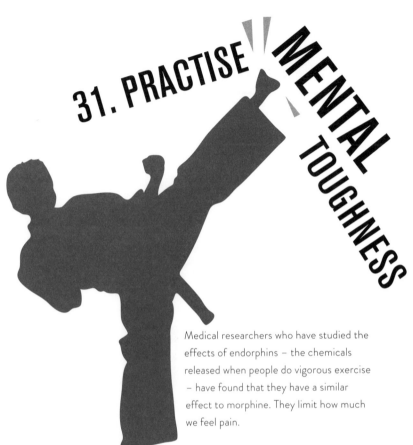

Medical researchers who have studied the effects of endorphins – the chemicals released when people do vigorous exercise – have found that they have a similar effect to morphine. They limit how much we feel pain.

This has a self-reinforcing effect on how much sportspeople and athletes can train, because it prevents them hurting when (in other circumstances) their bodies would be crying out for them to stop! For endurance athletes, such as long-distance cyclists, marathon runners and triathletes, this is particularly useful in their preparations for their events, but we can also apply this to life in general too.

If you want to improve your mental toughness in order to get what you really want in life – whether it's a more fulfilling relationship, a career change or a promotion – get into endurance sports. They are great for your body (you can lose weight without having to think so much about your diet), they're a chance to get out into the countryside, because most cities aren't big enough to cater for 120-km cycle rides or 5-km swims. And they send bucket-loads of endorphins coursing through your veins, dampening your experience of pain and making you feel euphoric.

Your friends will look at you with dumbstruck amazement and say they couldn't even run for the bus, never mind 21 km on a hot summer day, but what do they know? Every time you lace up your running shoes or clip in your cycle shoes, you're topping up your supply of mental toughness, just as if you were filling your car with fuel.

Other ways of building mental toughness include joining the military, getting sent to jail for a few months, going through an acrimonious divorce, being pursued by the tabloid press over a sex scandal or living in Brixton.

But I'd recommend endurance sport.

EVERY CALAMITY IS TO BE OVERCOME BY ENDURANCE.

Virgil (Roman poet)

32. VISUALISE PERFORMANCE

Visualising performance is something that athletes are taught to do, helping them to prepare psychologically for races, competitions and events. By putting themselves mentally in the middle of their event, whatever their discipline, they can summon up the emotions and sensations that they're going to feel on the day. So then, when the event comes around, it feels familiar to them rather than shocking or alien. It can help to reduce anxiety in athletes and help them to perform better, particularly in sports such as golf or cricket, where fine motor skills are needed – which can be thrown off by excessive nerves. Studies have shown that visualisation techniques for athletes have a measurable, concrete value. So it's certainly worth exploring how they can help you in achieving your life goals.

The technique works as a form of wish-fulfilment. You 'dream' of something happening; you desperately want it to happen, you imagine it happening. Unlikely as it may sound, the simple imaginative act of doing these things does make them more likely to happen.

> ## WHEN I WAS YOUNGER, I USED TO VISUALISE MYSELF SCORING WONDER GOALS.

Wayne Rooney (Manchester United striker and scorer of the best goal in 20 seasons of the Premier League)

Not only do these visualisations make you want to adapt a lifestyle that will make them more likely to happen, they encourage you to take steps to make them happen. So if you want to achieve that promotion, visualise yourself sitting in the corner office with your feet up on your boss's old desk. If you want to set up your own business, visualise your cafe full of happy customers. If you want to get married and have 2.4 children, picture these scenarios in your head.

Some cases in point: when Rory McIlroy was just 15 years old, his father and some of his friend placed bets adding up to a few hundred pounds that his son would win the British Open golf championship before he was 26 years old. When McIlroy won the Open on 20 July 2014, it marked the culmination of 10 years of visualisation on behalf of McIlroy senior and his friends, making them almost £200,000 richer! Formula 1 racing driver Lewis Hamilton's family placed a similar bet when he was 9 years old, which also came good.

Of course, not everyone can expect such fairy-tale endings, but there's no harm in trying.

PICTURE IT IN YOUR HEAD AND FIND A WAY OF MAKING IT HAPPEN.

33. USE POWER WORDS

All words have power, but some have more power than others. 'Jump!' can work well. 'Go!' is pretty good too. And, of course, all sports have their own vocabulary, which athletes learn as they learn the sport itself, helping them understand its inner workings. I'll explain how these words can be used to achieve your goals opposite. Here are some words which are quite specific to certain sports:

CADENCE

This is often used in cycling (though it can also apply to running). It means the speed at which the pedals are rotating – which is different to the speed of the wheels, because it depends which gear you're in. Good cadence is arguably more important for effective cycling than power alone.

THE NICK

This means the corner where the wall of a squash court meets the floor. Advanced players can aim the ball so that it hits the nick and rolls flat across the floor – an unplayable shot.

REVERSE SWEEP

This is a relatively new development in cricket, first played by Javed Miandad of Pakistan in the 1970s, where the batsman swaps the grip of the bat and plays left-handed (if he is right-handed) parallel to the ground. When played well, it takes the fielding team by surprise.

FADE AND DRAW

These two terms describe the path of a golf ball when it is hit with sidespin, meaning that it either curves to the left (draw), or to the right (fade).

Every field of human endeavour has its own vocabulary which you can use. They can help you to understand its inner workings and to succeed in that field. Away from the sports field, saying to yourself things like: 'Just do it!', 'Don't give up', 'I can, I will', 'Whatever it takes, I'm doing it', 'Get on with it!' can help with both more immediate goals, such as getting yourself out the door to go for that 10-km run, or longer-term projects such as finishing off decorating the hallway.

WORDS CAN LIGHT FIRES IN THE MINDS OF MEN.

Patrick Rothfuss (novelist)

34. LEARN

HOW TO PERFORM UNDER

PRESSURE

IT'S NOT ABOUT WHETHER YOU HAVE BUTTERFLIES IN YOUR STOMACH, IT'S ABOUT MAKING THEM ALL FLY IN THE SAME DIRECTION.

James Parrack
(Olympic swimmer and owner of
Blue Water Training Camp, Mallorca)

'Performing' takes many forms. For an athlete, it's usually about competitions, events and races, where there are often spectators, many other competitors and an easy way to judge the results. But giving a work presentation, even to a couple of colleagues, is a kind of performance too. Speaking at a wedding, a conference or a social gathering is as well.

Athletes know that they can count on up to 10 per cent better performance in an official competition than they will typically achieve in practice, because of the adrenalin that comes with the event. That's why so many world records are broken at the Olympic Games. As spectators, we love watching great athletes perform feats that we could not hope to emulate. It's entrancing and magical.

You can draw on this adrenalin and admiration in situations that are not sports-related too. Instead of dozens of runners, swimmers or cyclists jockeying around you, you have your colleagues, friends or members of the public watching you. Yes, it can be scary, but this is your moment to shine, so show them that you're unafraid of being in the spotlight.

Make that eulogy, PowerPoint presentation or best-man speech and do it well; try to enjoy being the centre of attention, no matter how brief or how much you might dread it. People love to watch each other perform and to excel – they will be urging you to do well, to overcome your inhibitions and to do something that they may be too frightened to do themselves.

Get up there and do it!

35.
BELIEVE IN YOURSELF

Psychology studies have shown that positive self-belief can have a measurable impact on sporting performance, being equal to illegal performance-enhancing drugs.

A report, published in *Scientific American Mind*, argues that positive self-belief and belief in a 'positive stereotype' can add as much as 5 per cent to an individual or team's performance – enough to be the difference between winning and losing. 'Preconceptions can boost both individual and group performance,' says Professor Alex Haslam of the University of Exeter. 'For example, if you belong to a group that is always exposed to the message "we are the best", then this can promote individual achievement.'

The research team concluded that, if it had more self-belief, the England football team could be the equal of the Germans. This may be stretching the point too far, on recent results, but the study certainly found that the theory applies not only to sport but many other areas in life. For example, a group of Asian women took a mathematics test in which some of them identified themselves as women, others as Asian. Those who put down 'Asian' produced significantly better results than those who called themselves 'women'. The study argued that this is due to the stereotype of women being poor at maths, but Asians excelling at the subject.

Back on the sports field, the breaking of the 4-minute mile is a case in point. On 6 May 1954, Roger Bannister became the first athlete to run a mile in less than 4 minutes, at a running track in Oxford, breaking a record that the medical profession and some scientists had said could result in potentially fatal injuries to the heart.

Yet within a year, 24 other athletes had also broken the 4-minute mile. Surely some of them were already fast enough runners to have done it before? The fact is that Bannister was the only one with the self-belief to manage it. His name is now world-famous, synonymous with an historic athletic achievement.

Whatever we try to achieve, self-belief is a crucial component, giving us a psychological lift which effort alone cannot provide. It goes back to the idea of wearing the work outfit for the job that you want rather than the job you have. If you think you can do it, you will do it.

> FIRST, DO ENOUGH TRAINING. THEN BELIEVE IN YOURSELF AND SAY: I CAN DO IT. TOMORROW IS MY DAY. AND THEN SAY: THE PERSON IN FRONT OF ME, HE IS JUST A HUMAN BEING AS WELL; HE HAS TWO LEGS, I HAVE TWO LEGS. THAT IS ALL. THAT IS MENTALLY HOW YOU PREPARE.

Haile Gebrselassie (Olympic Gold medallist runner and breaker of 27 world records)

36.
WANT
TO WIN

'Everything you do makes you faster, or slower,' a professional cyclist told me recently, as we prepared to ride up the Alpe d'Huez, one of the most iconic French ascents and the scene of many Tour de France dramas. He himself had ridden this route many times before. He had based himself in the region for weeks at a time, training for professional races either in France, nearby Switzerland or back in the United States, where he lived most of the time.

His will to win extended to his choice of breakfast cereal, the snacks he would take in his back pocket during the day, his detailed monitoring of his weight, his meticulous care of his bike ('A clean bike is a happy bike,' he would say. 'A dirty bike is more likely to go wrong.') and his plans for the forthcoming months and years.

For cyclists, a high-sugar diet is, paradoxically, an excellent thing while they're racing to provide quick-acting energy. But outside riding, his diet was carefully considered and monitored. 'There are only two ways to improve your cycling speed,' he told me. 'Increase your power or decrease your weight.'

Increasing cycling power is typically achieved, these days, by investing in a turbo trainer; a static machine which you can place your bike into, which then records your speed and can link to a TV screen or computer. So you can train all winter long, watching simulated images of Alpe d'Huez (or any one of hundreds of other routes).

Anyone wanting to win at their own discipline, whether sporting or not, would do well to emulate my cycling friend.

To succeed in your chosen field, narrow down the parameters of your ambition as much as possible. Figure out how to improve in those areas, then take your own advice (or pay for good advice, or hang around with experts in your chosen field) and go for it.

☞ Pay close attention to what you take on board
(whether food, information or experience).

☞ Look after your equipment and treat it with care.

☞ Increase your power.

☞ Go out and win.

WINNING IS THE SCIENCE OF BEING TOTALLY PREPARED.

George Allen Sr.
(American football coach)

Everyone has good days and bad days, but if you're a serious athlete or you're intent on realising a major goal in life, then you have to tread with care. In sporting competitions, there are often no second chances. The Olympic 100-metre final only happens once every four years and it takes less than ten seconds.

If you're aiming for a personal milestone such as a qualification, the same applies: you may get just the one shot. So you need to work out what causes these good and bad days and make sure that the big day coincides with a positive performance.

37. ACKNOWLEDGE YOUR PERFORMANCE UPS AND

Some factors that can influence both sporting and non-sporting performance are below. Think about what effect each of these things can have on your performance and the achieving of your goals. Then plan to reach the ideal state in advance of your event.

- Your health. Not just in terms of a definable illness – and avoiding illness on the big day – but your general state of health and energy levels. For instance, how you've been sleeping, or whether your digestion is working well; do you feel lethargic?

- If you drink alcohol, how does this affect your performance – not just the following day, but over the following week? Some people who depend on having a really sharp mind give up alcohol a month before a big event.

- Your diet. Overeating can be almost as damaging as having a hangover, leaving you sluggish and slow-witted. Eat wisely and not too much.

- Hydration. Make sure you drink enough water so that your body remains hydrated, especially in long meetings. Dehydration affects your energy levels, so you perform better when you've drunk enough water.

- Timing. A common mistake among athletes is to start off too quickly and then run out of puff. The same can be true in other fields. Pace yourself, think about the overall time it'll take and how to apportion your efforts. If you have a work deadline to make, think carefully about how long it's likely to need so that you don't end up rushing things and skimping on the final stages.

- Don't allow yourself to be discouraged. This can be hard when what you are doing is in the public gaze and you seem to be under-performing. Consider asking a mentor about your progress and what you can do better, then take their advice on board. Judge yourself according to your own standards – and those you respect – not by those of other people.

EXPECT THE BEST OF YOURSELF.
THEN DO WHAT IS NECESSARY
TO MAKE IT A REALITY.
Ralph Marston (motivational author)

It's easy to say that you should learn from your results, good and bad, as the quote opposite suggests. But what does that mean in practice? Bad results can be depressing and make you wish you hadn't bothered, or make you feel like giving up for good. Good results might just mean you carry on as you are. So what's there to learn from, then?

Here's what:

- Look back at your preparation. Could you have done more, or do something differently next time? That big presentation not go so well? Did you prepare thoroughly enough for the Q&A session?

- Was there a mis-match between your perception of the event – whether sporting or not – and the reality? Did you think it would be a breeze when, in fact, it was a hurricane? Did you do enough revision on that particular section?

- Did you underestimate the level of the competition? Next time, maybe you should adjust the standard that you're pitched against, get some more positive results and then return to this level. Perhaps you shouldn't have gone for that promotion? Was it too early in your career? Do you need more experience before climbing the next rung of the career ladder?

- Was it really so bad? If you compare your result with previous attempts at a similar discipline, was it much different? If not, then maybe you did just fine, but the overall standard of the event was higher than

38. LEARN FROM EVERY RESULT

> # IT'S FINE TO CELEBRATE SUCCESS BUT IT'S MORE IMPORTANT TO HEED THE LESSONS OF FAILURES.
>
> Bill Gates (Microsoft founder and one of the world's richest men)

you'd expected. If it really was, see the points opposite. If you think your conference speech was a flop, why not see if you can access a recording of the event to see how you really did?

I've run in competitions where there have been 12,000 competitors and felt great; I've finished my race and spent half an hour watching other people come in. But I've also raced in a field of 50 people and come second-to-last, feeling like a big fat lemon while everyone else has zoomed ahead of me. There was probably not much difference in my speed, but a world of difference in how the end result made me feel.

Like many people, I love to feel good – running a strong race, finishing in the top half of the field and coming out with a positive outlook. But you have to set yourself challenges and accept that, sometimes, you'll be one of the weakest in the field. It's a different kind of motivation but just as valuable.

39. OVERCOME OBSTACLES

In sport, the biggest obstacles that most people face are illness and injury. Whether they happen in training or during competition, the interruption to an athlete's career can be devastating. Particularly for those whose disciplines centre around major international events such as the Olympics or the football World Cup, where they may only get one chance in their lifetime.

The downsides of a bad illness or sporting injury are loss of condition and skills, having too much time on your hands, beginning to doubt whether you can rebuild your sports career (many people don't come back from serious injury) and loss of earnings. You may have to make crucial decisions over surgical procedures, with the risk of failure also ending your sporting career.

In a typical business career, losing your job can have a similar effect to a serious injury. It can certainly have a similar impact on your self-esteem and thoughts of your future prospects.

Here are some ways that professional athletes deal with injury that can be applied to careers:

- Allow yourself to feel the disappointment and frustration. The pain and upset of the situation shouldn't be ignored. But keep it short. In other words, allow yourself to feel angry that you were 'let go', but quickly

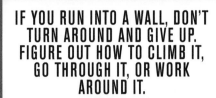

begin getting your CV up to date, make
some applications and get in touch with
contacts. Don't wallow.

· Come to terms with the situation and devise a strategy
  for the future, whether that is to return to your sport,
  your career or your relationship, or to move on.

· Be patient. Take the time to work on your CV; don't rush it.
  Consider job applications carefully; one good application is worth three
  half-hearted, rushed efforts.

· Take advice from professionals: they can help you to see your potential and how
  you are most likely to return to top form in the future. If you work in print media,
  is now the time to make the move into digital? To go freelance? To take a career
  break and travel? Work out what it is you really want to do now.

· Keep training or working on relevant projects connected with your career.
  Athletes who get injured can usually find exercises to do which keep them strong,
  in water for example. Keeping up to date with developments in your field fulfils a
  similar purpose.

· Stay determined to achieve future goals; going after them with the same passion
  you had before your injury, or loss of job. Recognise your achievements in light
  of the obstacles you've faced. Don't give up on a much-loved career if it takes you
  longer than you'd hoped to get another job.

40. DISCOVER YOUR OPTIMAL PERFORMANCE

Sportsmen and women are notoriously superstitious. If you watch footballers run onto the pitch, you will see some of them cross themselves several times, as though imploring God to bless their performance and help them win (How does He choose, if both sets of players seek his favours? Must it be a draw?). Others will perform a series of hops, others touch the grass or point to the heavens. In their memoirs, you will often read great lists of the things that athletes will do before big matches or events. They have a favourite dish, they wear 'lucky' socks, or perform some arcane ritual involving candles and pictures of Miley Cyrus.

One snooker player would retire to his hotel room for riotous sex with his wife during breaks in his big matches, with excellent results (although he died young).

Once you've reached a certain level with your training, your experience of big events and your knowledge of your sport and the competition, the only things that can account for a good or bad performance, in many athletes' minds, are these random factors and superstitions.

The rational sceptic in me would say it's all rubbish and that meticulous preparation, a great diet and a healthy lifestyle are the best guarantors of success in both sport and life. Whether it's a big match or an important exam, the best you can do for is eat well, look after yourself and prepare, prepare, prepare.

But the psychologist in me says: 'Hold on. If someone believes that crossing themselves when they run on the pitch will bring them good fortune, and that God will bless them (and not their opponents), then surely that can have a concrete effect.'

'Do what works for you' is a perfectly good approach. There are some marginal habits that many coaches would propose: wear clean, smart clothes (certainly a good idea in business, so why not in sport?); be courteous, polite and cool-headed; make sure you warm up (a mental warm-up ahead of a business meeting can be a good idea too – run through your pitch just before you step into the meeting room); and stay alert to changing conditions.

The more you test yourself, the more you'll know what will produce a great performance.

> **ACHIEVE SUCCESS IN ANY AREA OF LIFE BY IDENTIFYING THE OPTIMUM STRATEGIES AND REPEATING THEM UNTIL THEY BECOME HABITS.**

Charles J. Givens (financial writer)

41. RECOGNISE THE VALUE OF TEAMWORK

In team sports, the contribution of each member is clear to see. Managers and coaches also form a vital part of the effort. But even in individual sports, great athletes typically have teams of people behind them, adding expertise and experience, support and encouragement, from behind the scenes.

A tennis champion like Andre Agassi had perhaps 8–10 people, including different trainers for different disciplines, along with nutrition advisers, sports psychology experts, advisers to suggest match tactics and other members of his entourage who were there simply to keep him sane and grounded. And in a sport like cycling, a group can go much quicker than an individual, by sharing the effort and 'drafting' behind one another.

In our everyday lives, we all have friends, colleagues and acquaintances who play similar roles, contributing towards our goals and sharing the effort, even if we haven't stopped to consider it that way.

- Could you find a mentor in the workplace to advise you on your next step career-wise?
- When chatting with your children's teachers, or your gym instructor, do they have advice that could help you?
- Ask a bookshop assistant to suggest inspirational biographies.
- Consider hiring a life coach (or someone who's an expert in the field you're pursuing).
- Ask your partner to help you. Would they be prepared to shoulder more domestic tasks in order for you to study for a qualification? Could they listen to you running through your pitch in order for you to practise it?

People enjoy being part of a team effort and making a difference. It gives them a sense of progress and development. Getting married? Why not ask your florist aunt to make the table centrepieces? Your uncle is a recruitment consultant? What interview tips could he give you? Don't be afraid to ask for help. Create a team around you. Make it fun, and people will join in of their own accord!

❝ TEAMWORK: I FIND IT FASCINATING THAT A SNOWFLAKE, BY ITSELF, CAN BE SO DELICATE; BUT WHEN THEY TEAM UP, THEY CAN CLOSE DOWN AN ENTIRE CITY. ❞

Steve Maraboli
(author and behavioural scientist)

42. CHANNEL YOUR YOUR

COMPETITIVE SPIRIT

A healthy competitive spirit is vital for sportspeople to excel. To really commit yourself to a career in sport, you have to be driven by a desire to win. That same drive applies to many of the most successful people in business; those who can commit to a goal with absolute dedication and direct all of their energies to achieving it. A competitive spirit motivates us all to a degree. In the schoolroom we compete with our peers to get good grades; at work we compete for jobs.

Athletes approach competition by recognising the link between hard work, preparation and achievement. The competition is often with oneself: to perform better than in the past, to set a new personal best or to overcome personal challenges. This can feel just as satisfying as winning a public race in front of thousands. Certainly for the amateur sportsperson and for those who seek lessons from sporting achievement, the individual act – in competition with one's own past, demons, failures, hopes and dreams – is a powerful motivator.

Learning to channel competitive spirit is also about respect and consideration for others. Sport is, at best, a kind of family, in which everyone shares in each other's joy and pain. Winners and losers embrace at the end of a match and appreciate one another's efforts. If a colleague gets the promotion rather than you, you shake their hand.

So without diminishing the idea and value of winning, it's worth remembering Baron de Coubertin's motto for the Olympics: *Citius, Altius, Fortius* ('Faster, higher, stronger') alongside the second motto: 'The most important thing is not to win but to take part'. If you compete in a true competitive spirit, then you will always be rewarded.

"I VIEW MY STRONGEST COMPETITION AS MYSELF.

YOU'RE ALWAYS TRYING TO TOP YOURSELF, RATHER

THAN WORRYING ABOUT WHAT OTHER PEOPLE ARE DOING."

John C. Reilly
(American actor)

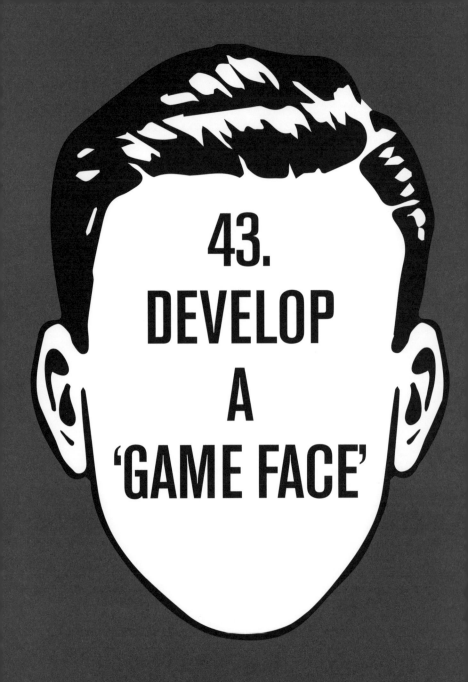

43.
DEVELOP
A
'GAME FACE'

There are two main definitions of 'game face'. It's either a 'confident swagger' that someone puts on when they're facing a big challenge, or else it's a 'neutral or serious expression', designed to conceal emotion. Whichever suits you best, this is a tactic developed in sport which can apply to pretty much anything. Negotiating a pay rise? Put on your game face. Telling your partner about your plans for yet another weekend away with your friends? Game face. Demanding a refund? Game face.

The basic idea is that human negotiations are perpetual games. There are winners and losers in individual transactions, even if the whole system remains in balance so that nobody actually wins or loses overall. You want a refund, but you don't want the business to go bankrupt because that would defeat the purpose.

Similarly, in sport, you want to win the point, win the game, but you also want the series to continue. A game face is a way of saying that you're engaging in the sport, in the deal. You're not walking away. Wearing your game face when asking for a pay rise is a way of letting your employer know that you'll be snapped up if you go elsewhere; that you're not afraid to get what you're worth.

The best game face comes from knowledge of your superior (or at least equal) position in the negotiation. If you don't have that, or think you don't, then you need to work on your acting skills!

THE GREAT THING ABOUT ATHLETICS
IS THAT IT'S LIKE POKER SOMETIMES:
YOU KNOW WHAT'S IN YOUR HAND, AND
IT MAY BE A LOAD OF RUBBISH, BUT
YOU'VE GOT TO KEEP UP THE FRONT.

Sebastian Coe
(British Olympic gold medallist
runner and politician)

44.
IGNORE NEGATIVE THOUGHTS

Much of the attraction with sport is that the outcome is uncertain. We watch (and participate) partly because there is tension, drama, anticipation and, finally, a conclusion, which may be both astonishing and breathtaking.

Athletes have to live with this uncertainty all their professional lives. No matter how good they have become at their sport, there may be a new, young athlete just about to supplant them, or their own abilities may suddenly desert them. Dwelling on these potential future disasters is useless for athletes. It only inhibits their progress and cramps their style. Some, sadly, crack under the pressure. Away from the track, if we were to go around thinking that our partner was about to go off with someone else, all the time and without good reason, that would do our mental health no good at all. If you worry that your boss is planning to sideline you at every turn – without concrete evidence of this – then it will hinder your performance at work and your anxieties will eat away at your self-esteem; it's a vicious circle.

For the majority of athletes, achieving a positive outlook and ignoring negative thoughts is part of their professional lives.

Here are some tips to achieve it in yours:

- You are not your thoughts. You have a choice whether to believe them.
- Having negative thoughts is a form of emotional insurance you want to avoid at all costs. You can prove yourself right by acting negatively, to bring about a negative prediction.
- Stop catastrophising. Write down a) the worst-case scenario, b) the best outcome and c) the most realistic outcome. Act accordingly.
- Accept that you can't control everything in your life, much as an athlete can only be responsible for their own performance. That said, you can shape the course of events by preparing and taking good care of yourself.

It's important to distinguish between performance goals and outcome goals. Swimmers, for example, have no control over the temperature of the water, the weather conditions, their opponents, etc. so they ignore them. Importantly, they have no control over the clock. It just starts and stops according to electrical impulses. They can control what they eat, their mental preparation, positive thinking, and a hundred things that affect how well they perform – their strength and conditioning, flexibility, stroke technique, the start, length of stroke and effort.

Whether we're athletes or not, if we give the performance we know we can, by focusing on what we can control, the outcome will be what we want.

IF YOU ACCEPT THE EXPECTATIONS OF OTHERS, ESPECIALLY NEGATIVE ONES, THEN YOU NEVER WILL CHANGE THE OUTCOME.
Michael Jordan
(greatest basketball player in history)

45. CHANNEL PERFORMANCE ANXIETY

Competing in any sporting activity is a kind of performance. You're on show, even if the only audience is your opponent in a tennis match. This public display is an integral part of sport: the aesthetics of your dress, your movement, the grammar of your body language, the attitude you present and your reaction to winning or losing.

Some people find this public scrutiny unbearable in many parts of their lives – speaking at big events, playing musical instruments in front of a crowd, etc. – but can find the confidence to play sports in public. Take the millions who run city marathons, for example.

Once you've had that experience of a public sporting performance, take it as a precedent: channel the feeling of overcoming your anxiety and apprehension before the event, and the strength you gained from overcoming your doubts and fears, into realising your life goals.

Here are some tips from sport performance:

· You will perform around 10 per cent better in a competitive environment than when training by yourself. Apply this principle to other fields in life, so that, by thinking like an athlete, you consistently out-perform. Challenge yourself. Say yes to that new project that will test your skills. Apply for that promotion. Ask that man out.

· When you enter a bar or restaurant, sit at the middle table where you can be seen by everyone. Hold the stage like a sporting superstar. People will be drawn to you and you'll have a better evening. Try it!

· Treat business or social negotiations like a public spectacle. You're in a game which people are paying to watch, so give them their money's worth. Put on a show.

· Remember that people respond well to genuine effort, skill and application. People, more often than not, want to help you get ahead. Work out those who don't and act accordingly.

ONE OF THE GREATEST DISCOVERIES A MAN MAKES, ONE OF HIS GREAT SURPRISES, IS TO FIND HE CAN DO WHAT HE WAS AFRAID HE COULDN'T DO.

Henry Ford (industrialist)

46.
MANAGE STRESS

Because they are so dependent on their bodies to work properly in order to succeed, athletes pay constant attention to keeping themselves in shape, well fed and rested, supple and strong.

The process of doing all these things, which will typically include elements of massage, physiotherapy and general relaxation therapies, will combine to de-stress athletes, simply as a matter of course. The links between physical and mental stress and poor performance are so clear that any athlete or coach will take steps to prevent it or, if it occurs, to remedy it.

Outside of sport, stress is just as much an obstacle to good performance and results. Company directors are often under pressure to deliver financial results, taking little account of the personal costs of stress in the workplace.

Developments like 'zero hours' contracts mean that workers have less and less job security; housing, energy and travel costs are rising faster than wages; the pressures of maintaining relationships, bringing up children, caring for elderly relatives... all of these can be deeply stressful.

A possible solution for many people is to think like an athlete and build stress relief into your daily routine. For some this will be through sport itself, exercising both body and mind, with its consequent endorphin production.

But equally it could be through entertainment (cinema, theatre, concerts, gigs), meeting with friends, walking in the park, eating out or shopping for clothes.

The point is to make the connection between your state of mind and the proportion of stress and relaxation in your life, to ensure that they remain in balance.

> REST IS NOT IDLENESS, AND TO LIE SOMETIMES ON THE GRASS UNDER TREES ON A SUMMER'S DAY, LISTENING TO THE MURMUR OF THE WATER, OR WATCHING THE CLOUDS FLOAT ACROSS THE SKY, IS BY NO MEANS A WASTE OF TIME.

John Lubbock (author)

47. LISTEN TO YOUR BODY

Like an expensive musical instrument, or a supercomputer for a company, an athlete's body is their most precious asset. And just like any object with many moving parts, which is regularly called upon to perform to its full extent, it can go wrong.

For athletes, detecting the difference between the strains and pulls that they should expect in training and a genuine injury is crucial. The great majority of pains are beneficial – indeed sports trainers talk about 'breaking down the muscle' in order that it should be built up again stronger than before. For the gym-goer, 'feeling the burn' is a routine expression.

The danger signs are where the body registers pain in places that shouldn't have it, or where a muscle or tendon starts to tear (such as a hamstring). When this happens, athletes understand that they may have to stop training or playing sport altogether for some days, weeks or even months.

This can be a devastating decision to reach. Even a world-class sportsman like Brazil's Neymar had to miss the World Cup semi-final because he picked up an injury. He sat on the bench next to his teammates, but knew he was unfit to play.

The parallels in non-sporting life are often related to exhaustion. Over-work or lack of sleep can cause us to under-perform, meaning that our reactions are slower and we're less able to handle complex tasks.

Like athletes, we need to distinguish between the routine and the exceptional, the pain of training (the everyday strains) and the longer-term, debilitating injury. Sometimes we really do have to stop what we're doing and take a break.

Most athletes have someone to advise them on how their body is performing and the severity of any injury. Non-athletes lack this constant, on-hand expertise, so it's worth trying to develop a sense of our own physical limits and what constitutes an injury which would keep us 'off games'. If your back twinges, is it worth seeing a physio before the pain gets too severe? If you're feeling mentally low, could it be worth going to see your GP or a counsellor before depression sets in? If you're in tears on a Sunday afternoon, perhaps it's time to change job? Learning an awareness of our bodies and striving to get this balance right could mean the difference between a couple of days' rest and a much-longer enforced absence from work and social activities. So stay alert!

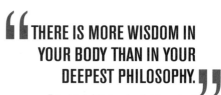

THERE IS MORE WISDOM IN YOUR BODY THAN IN YOUR DEEPEST PHILOSOPHY.

Friedrich Nietzsche (philosopher)

48. LISTEN TO YOUR HEAD

THE MORE DECISIONS YOU ARE FORCED TO MAKE ALONE, THE MORE YOU ARE AWARE OF YOUR FREEDOM TO CHOOSE.

Thornton Wilder (playwright and novelist)

Sometimes, the body feels weak but the head says go; or the body feels strong but the head says no. Athletes have to submit to certain routines which aren't always in parallel with what their bodies are telling them. For example, their coach will push them to do extra hill reps when they're already feeling shattered, because it will extend their stamina and replicate the feelings that they'll have during a race. Sometimes the best advice for an athlete is to stop doing what they're enjoying because otherwise they'll burn out. This is known as 'overtraining' – sometimes caused by not allowing yourself enough recovery time between events. At other times an athlete will have to cut back their training so they have enough energy, otherwise known as 'tapering'. In the weeks before a key race or competition you have to dramatically reduce your training so that you have enough energy on the day to perform.

Timing for big events is often key. Olympic champion runner Mo Farah withdrew from the 2014 Commonwealth Games in Glasgow at the last minute. Since he still expected to compete in Zurich 3 weeks later, it was perhaps a rational rather than physical decision.

Pressure from friends, relations and colleagues can direct us towards all kinds of activities that may be in our best interests, even if our bodies are unwilling (or vice versa). So it's up to us to trust our instincts and our intelligence and make decisions based on long-term goals.

For example, on the 'go' side:

Always take an opportunity to spend time in wilderness. Even if it means a long journey, it resets your body clock and connects you with nature.

Swimming, especially outdoors, is a great balm to the body and soul. Ignore your physical dread of the cold and wet and trust your head.

And on the 'no' side:

Car boot sales are almost always disappointing and a waste of time.

Musicals are generally overpriced, over-rated and may send you to sleep.

49. PAIN AS EFFORT

Cyclists speak of their pain thresholds like other sportspeople speak of medals or cups. 'He has a fantastic ability to endure pain,' one cyclist will say of another.

Along with long-distance running, round-the-world yachting and contact sports like rugby and American football, cycling is symbolic of the glorious masochism of extreme sport.

Riding at full pace for 4 or 5 hours, racing up insane gradients in the baking midday heat and careering down steep, narrow cobbled streets at 65 km/h is close to madness.

On the other hand, for those who have done it, or been somewhere close to it, the adrenalin and sense of living on the edge, being a millisecond away from disaster for hour after hour while hurting so much, makes the world a brighter, more vivid place.

AND REWARD

Having done major cycle tours,
the dangers and threats of a corporate
boardroom seem ludicrously tame by contrast.
Relationship strife is merely a distraction that a few minutes'
dedicated effort can often (hopefully) resolve. Work projects demanding
intense concentration for a couple of hours begin to seem like a breeze.

These are some of the benefits that taking part in relatively high-level
sport can bring. They are harder to explain or to comprehend in the
abstract. But the lesson remains valid: enduring pain for a prolonged
period can be hugely positive.

> ## PAIN IS TEMPORARY, PRIDE IS FOR EVER.

New Zealand swim team motto

50. SCHEDULE PHYSICAL AND MENTAL BREAKS

"DON'T GIVE UP ON YOUR DREAMS. SLEEP MORE."

Rebel Circus magazine

All of us, athletes or not, have to replenish our bodies and minds through rest. When you're demanding a lot of your body, as an athlete, or a lot of your mind, in a business venture or academic study for example, the need for recuperation is all the greater. The digital age has chipped away at our willingness and ability to have breaks, however. People commonly report that they are sleeping less, as they wake frequently in the night to check their messages or updates on social media. We are rarely ever out of signal, and therefore never away from the tentacular arms of our colleagues and managers, our friends updating us with their activities or the relentless pulse of news from a thousand different outlets.

So, once again, it's instructive to look at the schedule of a professional athlete. They will train for a couple of hours in the morning, eat, then sleep. An afternoon session will be followed by more sleep. Then an evening session, light meal, and to bed.

I remember thinking how luxurious and even magical it would be to do sports and sleep all day. How carefree an existence, how nurturing. And every so often, I've had a chance to get into that routine, when scuba diving on a 'live-aboard' yacht, for example, where you may do four dives per day, punctuated by sleep.

For people in the creative industries, sleep is a great source of mental nutrition: 'sore labour's bath, balm of hurt minds, great nature's second course, chief nourisher in life's feast...' as Macbeth put it.

Few businesses allow you to sleep at work, but if you're given the choice (or you work from home) then take it.

51. TIME YOUR HOLIDAYS CAREFULLY

Athletes commonly pace themselves in terms of 4-year periods, in between Olympic Games, or World Championships, or similar major events at which they need to reach peak performance.

This means that they also time their holidays to coincide with the least pressured points in their calendars, most obviously just following a big event. This allows them time to regroup, celebrate or forget their results and stock up on energy and motivation for the years ahead. For those of us who are not professional athletes, most of our holiday breaks follow a different rhythm, centring on an Easter, summer and Christmas break.

But if you have a life goal that you're desperate to achieve, why not cast aside these conventional breaks and instead follow the athlete's pattern, scheduling a holiday to come after a major event and working through the times when most other people are away? Treat a day when others are on holiday as a golden opportunity. Then take a break when everyone else is working to reward yourself.

This would have all kinds of benefits. You'd be able to concentrate more on realising your ambition during regular holidays, with more peace and quiet. You'd benefit from cheaper travel and accommodation rates if

MY NORMAL LIFE IS LIKE BEING ON HOLIDAY.

Valentino Rossi
(nine-time Grand Prix world motorcycle champion)

you're outside school dates. And you'll gain a greater sense of purpose through forfeiting something that others enjoy. Your sacrifice will gain value in comparison. Even small breaks like weekends can be valuable time for you to pursue your goals. If you get used to this, you may fancy self-employment (or maybe you already are), where you have ultimate control of your time.

An athlete has, in a way, the ultimate self-employment. They're so good at being free of society's restrictions that everyone pays them to stay that way. So it's like a never-ending holiday.

52. USE TECHNOLOGY

THE NUMBER ONE BENEFIT OF INFORMATION
TECHNOLOGY IS THAT IT EMPOWERS PEOPLE
TO DO WHAT THEY WANT TO DO. IT LETS PEOPLE
BE CREATIVE. IT LETS PEOPLE BE PRODUCTIVE.
IT LETS PEOPLE LEARN THINGS THEY DIDN'T
THINK THEY COULD LEARN BEFORE.

Steve Ballmer (former Microsoft CEO)

Watch a group of runners, cyclists or even swimmers training. The chances are that most of them have computers on their wrists or in pockets, recording their every move, their heart-rate, their altitude and calories burned. Software packages and online apps such as Strava will let them compare results with their friends and strangers, hold mini-competitions and compile all kinds of comparative data. Video systems like GoPro allow athletes to look back at their performances later on, while other software packages are designed to offer training modules, nutrition advice and an extraordinary array of services. It has radically changed the equipment that sportspeople use and wear.

Whatever your goals in life, seek out ways to harness new technology to help you do the same.

For example:

- Find others who share your passion, either nearby or anywhere in the world. Google them, join online communities, swap ideas and suggestions.

- Look up examples of people pursuing your passion on YouTube. It's incredible how encyclopaedic that website has become. People learn extraordinary new skills from it.

- Seek out a software programme that will offer helpful training tips in your field, with a schedule to follow and a guide to making improvements. We're all becoming more familiar with online learning, so don't shy away from it. Embrace the new!

- Find out whether there is a technological means of measuring your progress and giving you feedback. Use 'Big data' tools to improve your performance and give you comparative details.

The wonder of new technology is that it can help us outperform, raise our standards, introduce us to new challenges and opportunities and make learning fun. And if it seems impersonal, then use it to find fellow enthusiasts. The possibilities are infinite.

If you're truly determined to realise a goal, you have to be disciplined beyond the realms of hobbyism and into the world of professionalism. If you want to set up your own business, for example, you're going to need to spend time researching the market to make sure there is a niche for your product or service; find a financial backer; draw up a business plan... and that's even before you've started offering your service or making your product. That's just the first few, preparatory steps.

Athletes, of course, treat their training as a job, because it is, in effect, their career and they can be as well remunerated from it (indeed better) as most regular jobs. They use all the tools available to them to excel: scientific preparation, expert coaching, psychological advice, tactical awareness, dietary and nutritional programmes and performance measurement, among others.

Just like a business with an array of computer and software systems, they approach fitness and performance from every angle, to produce the optimum result.

53. TREAT YOUR

To give your non-sporting passion the same degree
of professional commitment:

- Make sure you work set hours on your project.

- Set deadlines for specific tasks.

- Use software tools such as spreadsheets to monitor your progress.

- Compare your progress with that of others in a similar position.

- Think about hiring the right people to give you professional advice,
  encouragement and suggestions on how to improve.

Sportspeople are great role models for anyone seeking to take their passion
more seriously, because that is what almost all of them have done.

From childhood races and competitions with fellow schoolkids through
local, regional and national competition, they have reached a point
of excellence equivalent to a high-flying business career, simply by
concentrating on getting better at something they love.

Be inspired!

PASSION AS A JOB

**PASSION IS ONE GREAT FORCE THAT UNLEASHES
CREATIVITY, BECAUSE IF YOU'RE PASSIONATE ABOUT
SOMETHING, THEN YOU'RE MORE WILLING TO TAKE RISKS.**
Yo-Yo Ma (cellist)

54. IT'S A MARATHON,

Even a sprint is a marathon, when it comes to preparation. A sprinter has to spend years conditioning their muscles and body to explode out of the blocks. If you visit a running track when sprinters are around, you'll see the meticulous preparation they put into every part of their training, from drills to reps.

Psychologically, all athletes treat their disciplines as marathons. They know that achieving great things will take years of their lives, as they build strength, endurance, speed and skill.

To emulate them, think about adopting some of the world's top athletes' practices in their preparation:

- Train harder and longer than everyone else, like footballers David Beckham or Lionel Messi. Practice is not a chore, it's a process of improvement that never stops. Always keep yourself abreast of new technology; keep your skills up to date throughout your career.

- Make sure you have the right equipment and that you take good care of it, as professional cyclists do. Understand how it works, how to maintain it and repair it and how to get the best performance from it. Always be nice to those around you; you never know when you'll need someone.

NOT A SPRINT

· Pace yourself so that you're as strong at the end of your 'race' (which could be a period of many years) as you are at the beginning and in the middle. Conserve energy when appropriate by steeling yourself for endurance. Don't burn out before your business or career really takes off; learn when to rest and when to get your head down.

· Pay attention to nutrition, throughout your 'race'. Just as runners and cyclists take care to load themselves with energy drinks and snacks before and during a race, you need to think about what is fuelling you through your programme, whether it's ideas, feedback, appreciation by others or new discoveries. Take good care of yourself and surround yourself with the right people in order to achieve your life goals.

> I've learned that finishing a marathon isn't just an athletic achievement. It's a state of mind; a state of mind that says anything is possible.

John Hanc (athletics writer)

55.
BUILD
YOUR
RESIL-
IENCE

> # A GOOD HALF OF THE ART
> # OF LIVING IS RESILIENCE.

Alain de Botton (philosopher)

Athletes build resilience through tailored training regimes. They use resistance techniques such as elasticated ropes to strengthen their muscles as they pull against them and choose steep hill gradients to run or cycle up, improving their strength and resilience. Mentally, too, athletes need to be inured to disappointment and hardened to the shocks of failure. It's difficult to replicate this in training so, for most, resilience to setbacks comes from the heat of competition and the cold reality of injury, setting them back and getting them to reassess life.

To build sporting resilience into your life, try the following:

• Put your ideas into the public domain, or at least test them out on your friends. Tell them your business plan and then be ready to debate its merit.

• Enter some kind of competition which will give you a benchmark by which to judge your efforts. If you've always aspired to being a bestselling author, try participating in NaNoWriMo (National Novel Writing Month).

• Teach young people to do what you're learning to do yourself. Teaching is (according to one of my best teachers at school) the best way of learning something. It's also a stiff test of your own understanding and confidence. If you're about to pitch an idea, run it past your toughest critics: your children.

• Extend yourself beyond your comfort zone. Read more widely. Travel somewhere to pursue your passion. Meet fellow enthusiasts. Go to that work conference in Brazil. Who knows who you'll meet and what you'll learn?

Just keep on doing what you're doing for long enough and you'll gain a certain degree of resilience. And many athletes are great examples of that.

56. TAKE INSPIRATION

These days, it's hard to move without bumping into an inspiring athlete. Since the Olympics, the Glasgow Commonwealth Games, the Tour de France in Yorkshire, the global excellence of the Premier League football teams, not to mention a British winner of Wimbledon at last, the regular flow of mesmerising British achievement in sport defies belief. Public sporting activities in the UK have increased exponentially as a result, bringing an enormous boost to the country's health and well-being.

In June 2014, I took part in the Hackney Half Marathon. There were more than 12,000 entrants haring around a course which took in the central London borough's various parks, famous old streets and the new Olympic park from 2012 with its iconic athletics stadium and vast swimming centre. Inspiring indeed.

Sportspeople are more open than ever before to the idea of acting as mentors, coaches and advisers, because they can use new technology to do so. You can follow them on Twitter, see their videos on YouTube and then get to meet them at all kinds of sporting events. Recently I did a swimming class with Karen Pickering, who swam for Great Britain for 9 years and won countless medals.

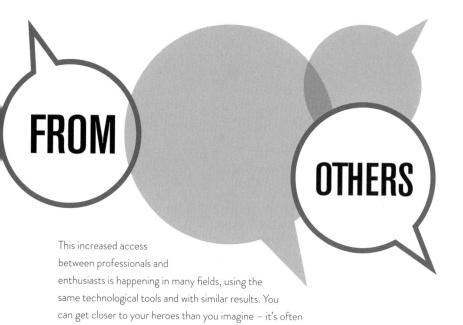

FROM

OTHERS

This increased access
between professionals and
enthusiasts is happening in many fields, using the
same technological tools and with similar results. You
can get closer to your heroes than you imagine – it's often
just a case of knowing where to look and being persistent.

Here are some tips:

• Follow people you admire on Twitter and Facebook.

• Watch out for their personal appearances, usually when they're
  promoting an event, product or book.

• Read their biographies and take note of their training or
  business techniques, whether it's Andre Agassi or
  Alan Sugar.

• Go to the same training centres as them to
  pick up similar skills, whether it's a triathlon
  training camp or a cookery class run by a pro.

A MAN ONLY LEARNS IN TWO WAYS, ONE BY READING, AND THE OTHER BY ASSOCIATION WITH SMARTER PEOPLE.

Will Rogers
(American cowboy, humorist and actor)

57. UNDERSTAND WHAT WORKS FOR YOU

It's part psychology, part physiology. Some people thrive on following orders, others like to stick to their own path. Getting this balance right can mean the difference between a gold medal and finishing way down the table; between success or burn-out.

For several years triathletes Alistair and Jonny Brownlee were competing for the top spot in Olympic events and world championships. But then, in 2014, Jonny found that he was training too hard and suffered as a result. 'I needed a coach that would get me to back off, rather than one that would make me work harder,' he said. A good coach will spot the signs of overtraining. Different training techniques and nutrition advice can help to correct these issues, once identified. A good life coach can help you achieve similar acts of rebalancing and adjustment as you pursue your life goals. But for a DIY approach, here are some top tips:

- If you find yourself wondering 'why am I doing this?' Then give yourself a break and come back to it later.
- Take your qualities and attributes and how they fit you in certain fields into account when making life decisions.

Most importantly, different things will suit you at different points in your lifetime. In your twenties, you may not want to put your all into buying your first home – or it might be your top priority. It may be that you want to throw yourself into your career in your thirties or you might decide to start a family and take a step back. It might be that this is the perfect time for you to take the plunge and set up your own business – or it might not. No matter what the challenge, no matter where you are in life, there are always lessons to be learned from the way in which athletes live their lives. Focus on your goal and go for it!

> THE GREATEST DISCOVERY OF MY GENERATION IS THAT A HUMAN BEING CAN ALTER HIS LIFE BY ALTERING HIS ATTITUDES.

William James (American philosopher)

ABOUT
THE
AUTHOR

An avid but ungarlanded
athlete, David Nicholson devotes most
of his energy to sport. In between training
and events, he writes about sport (and business,
politics, travel and technology) for UK and
international media. He lives in London, next door
to the mighty Arsenal Football Club – an endless
source of inspiration and entertainment.
Look up his work at:
www.freelancejournalist.co.uk
follow him on:
www.twitter.com/fljournalist or like www.
facebook.com/freelancejournalist.co.uk.

ACKNOWLEDGEMENTS

Thanks to James Parrack at BEST Swim Centre for advice and comments, Neil Aitken at Embrace Sports for inspiration and Rory Manning at rj-fitness.com for motivation.

Thank you to my publisher Kate Pollard for approaching me and making this happen, to Kajal Mistry for her help and assistance and to Jim Green for his artistic vision and design.

DAVID NICHOLSON

Think Like an Athlete by David Nicholson

First published in 2015 by Hardie Grant Books

Hardie Grant Books (UK)
5th & 6th Floors
52–54 Southwark Street
London SE1 1UN
www.hardiegrant.co.uk

Hardie Grant Books (Australia)
Ground Floor, Building 1
658 Church Street
Melbourne, VIC 3121
www.hardiegrant.com.au

British Library Cataloguing-in-Publication Data. A catalogue record
for this book is available from the British Library.

ISBN 978-1-74270-930-7

Illustrations on pages 42, 45, 55, 68, 92, 101, 104, 106 and 124 © 2003-2014
Shutterstock, Inc. All rights reserved.

Illustrations on pages 11, 23 and 62 ©2014 iStockphoto LP. All rights reserved.

Publisher: Kate Pollard
Senior Editor: Kajal Mistry
Editors: Nicky Jeanes, Louise Francis & Simon Davis
Cover and Internal Design: Jim Green
Colour Reproduction: p2d

Printed and bound China by 1010 Printing International Limited

10 9 8 7 6 5 4 3 2 1